STEVE BRIGHT

Printed and Published in Great Britain
by D. C. THOMSON & CO. LTD.,
185 Fleet Street, London, EC4A 2HS
© D. C. THOMSON & CO., LTD., 2008
ISBN 978 1 84535 318 6   EAN 9 781845 353186

I WISH I WAS...
WHICH GENIE CHARACTER SUITS YOU?

1. Mum tells you to clear up your room. Do you...

IT'S ABOUT TIME WE HAD SOME PROPER HELP, SOMEONE WHO CAN ASSIST ME IN BEING AS LAZY AS POSSIBLE!!

GENIE, I WISH FOR A ROBOT ASSISTANT!!

a) get someone else to do it for you,

b) order chocolate cake and biscuits from room service with a large drink on the side,

c) get on with it and do everyone else's as well?

2. What's your favourite type of hat?

a) You'd never wish for anything other than a woolly one rolled up at the bottom. Warm in winter...and summer.

b) For a dashing look, you can't beat a flying-style helmet with goggles.

c) The fez style always makes the wearer look very creative (which they usually

3. You are on a mission to save the world from being overrun by the jelly creatures from planet Bifidus Digestivans. The jelly creatures have you surrounded. Do you...

a) get someone else to conjure up a nucleo-blaster jelly-fragmenter,

b) order some ice cream and look for some jelly to go with it,

c) produce a nucleo-blaster jelly-fragmenter to save the day?

4. Someone (!) has wished you into the court of Louis XVI, the king of France. Do you...

a) start wishing mice into everyone's big hairdos,

b) see if Marie Antoinette's made any cake,

c) wait to see where you're going next, with your fingers crossed?

HEE HEE, THIS IS GREAT, GENIE! I DON'T NEED TO EVER DO ANYTHING EVER AGAIN!!

EXCEPT EAT CAKE!!

LULA, YOU WERE LAZY TO START WITH!! THIS HAS MADE YOU WORSE!!

5. There's a chance to go wind-surfing in Antarctica, head-to-head with Sigmund Yellowfeet the penguin Surf Champion. Do you...

a) make sure you have a secret fan built on to the back of your board for extra varoomsh,

b) suggest that a voyage round the local boating pond might be a better idea,

c) check to see where you can get a self-propelled wind-surfer?

YOU HAVE BEEN GRANTED ONE WISH - TO BE IN MY OWN GENIE. ANSWER THIS LOT AND YOU'LL KNOW IF YOU SHOULD BE CLIVE, LULA OR BRIAN THE GENIE.

6. Your favourite way to relax is?

a) Get someone else to do all the chores, (so like all the rest of the time...).

b) A long lie, a leisurely breakfast and maybe some hot chocolate for elevenses.

c) Not having to conjure up dancing poodles, violin-playing washing machines or making the dodo unextinct.

7. You're really, really, really bored. So bored that double Trigonometry with Mr Fruitbat seems appealing. There's only one thing to do...

AT SCHOOL!

a) wish you were somewhere else, anywhere else, even inside a dinosaur's gizzard,

b) lie back, relax and tuck into a light snack,

c) get worried because you know that in about 5 minutes you're going to be somewhere really, really strange - like inside a dinosaur's gizzard.

8. What's your ultimate wish EVER?

a) The next one you can come up with.

b) To wear a hat in peace and have people talking in awe about your magnificent nose.

c) Me, make a wish, that's not how it works...

Mostly As:
You're obviously Lula, aren't you? We had to say that or you'd have gone in the huff, wouldn't you? Or wished us all turned into earthworms... with handlebar moustaches and cheese-flavoured shorts.

Mostly Bs:
Clive is the dog for you. You don't mind having a bit of fun, but you don't want to get totally carried away. And, more importantly, you always know where the chocolate biscuits are.

Mostly Cs:
You are a bit of a Genie. You always get things done — for yourself and for other people. But you don't mind, really. Or maybe just a bit when things get extraordinarily silly!

Mostly Ds:
There were no D answers so you are obviously not a real person. You are a jelly creature from the planet Bifidus Digestivans! ARRGH!

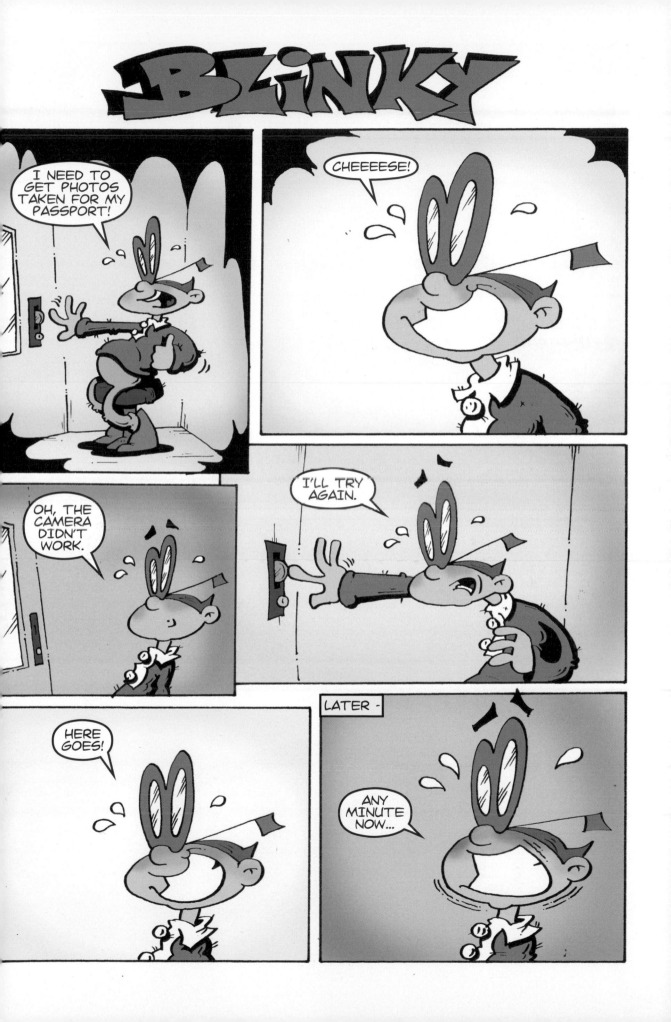

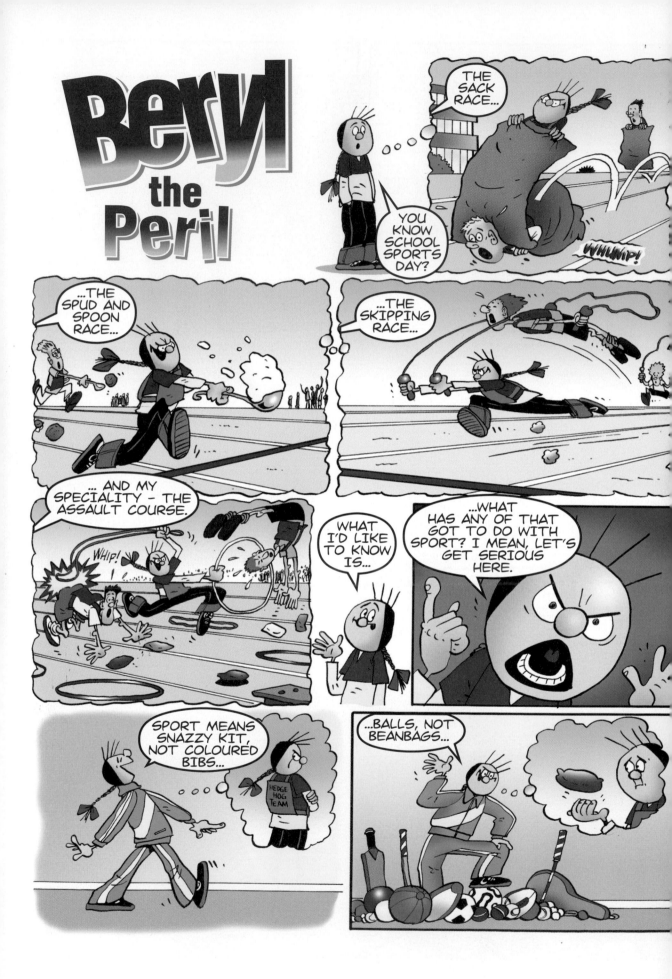

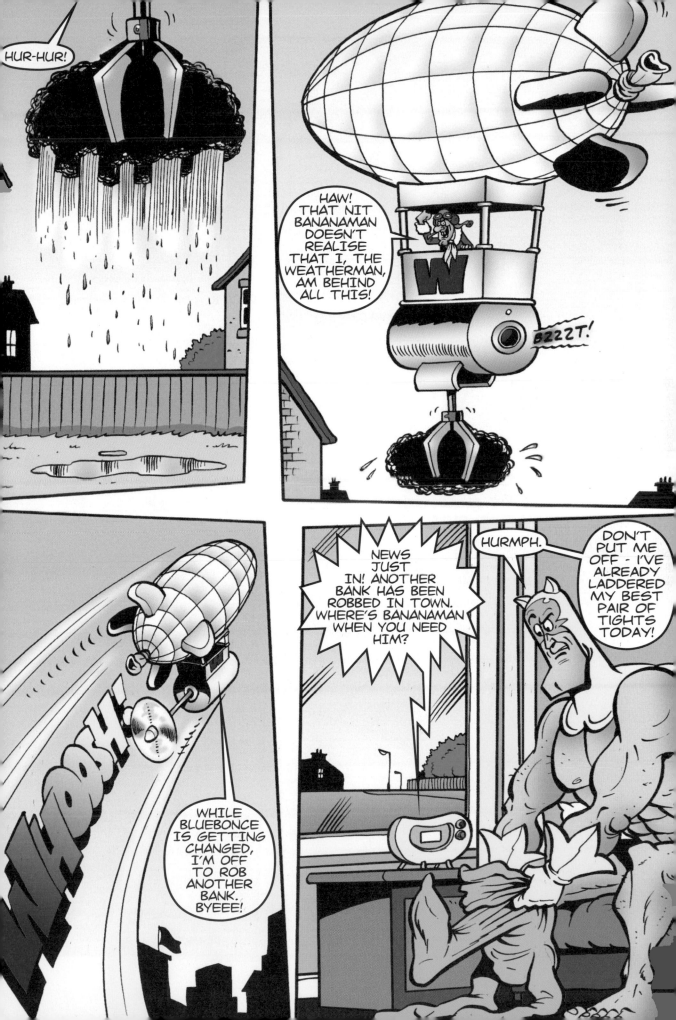

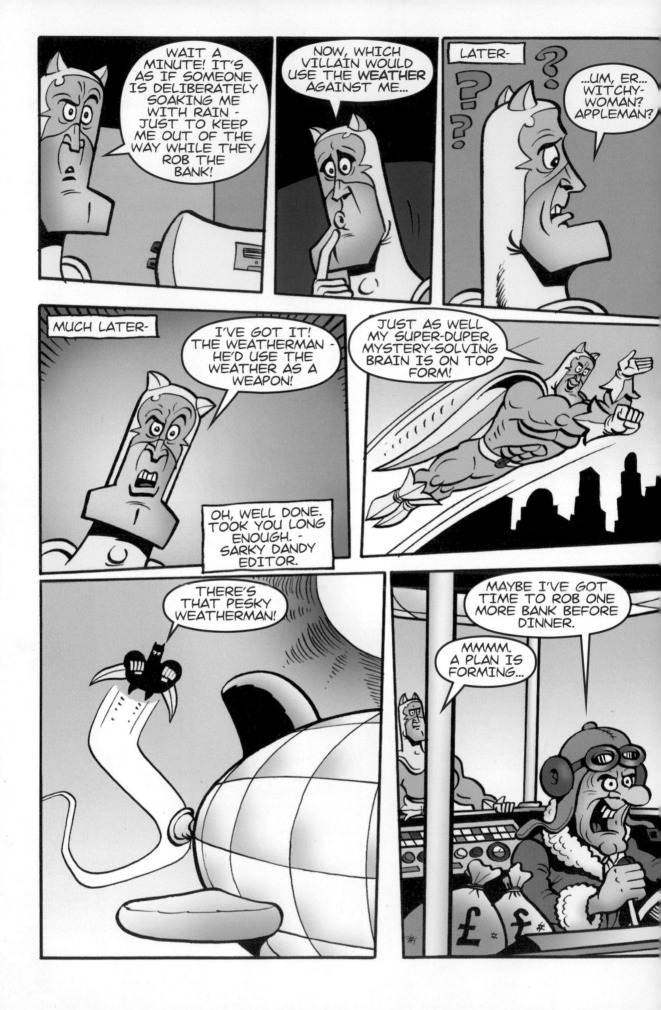

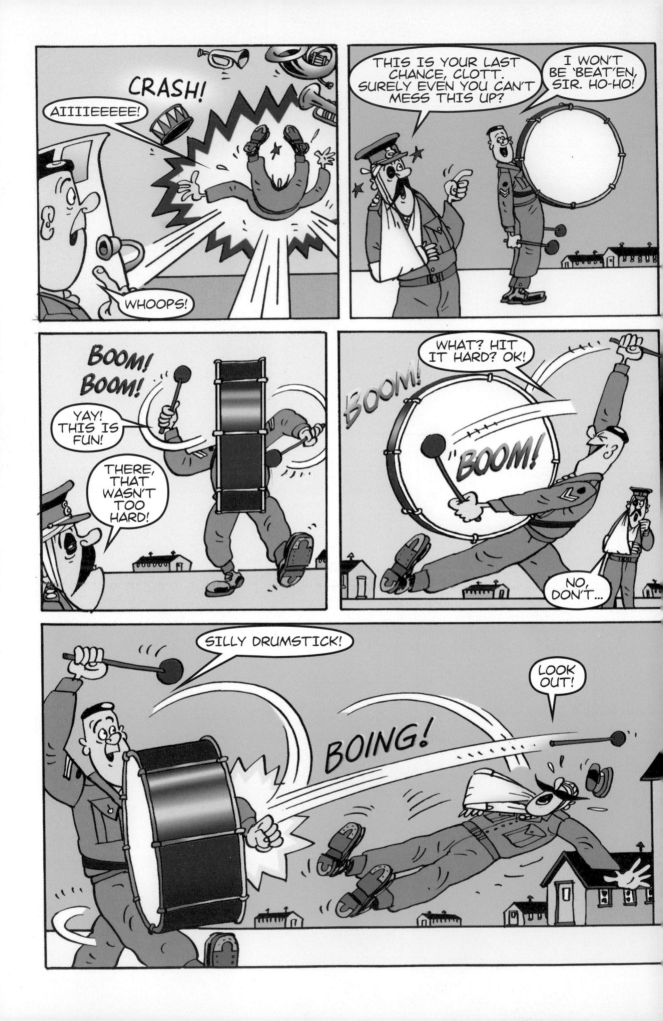

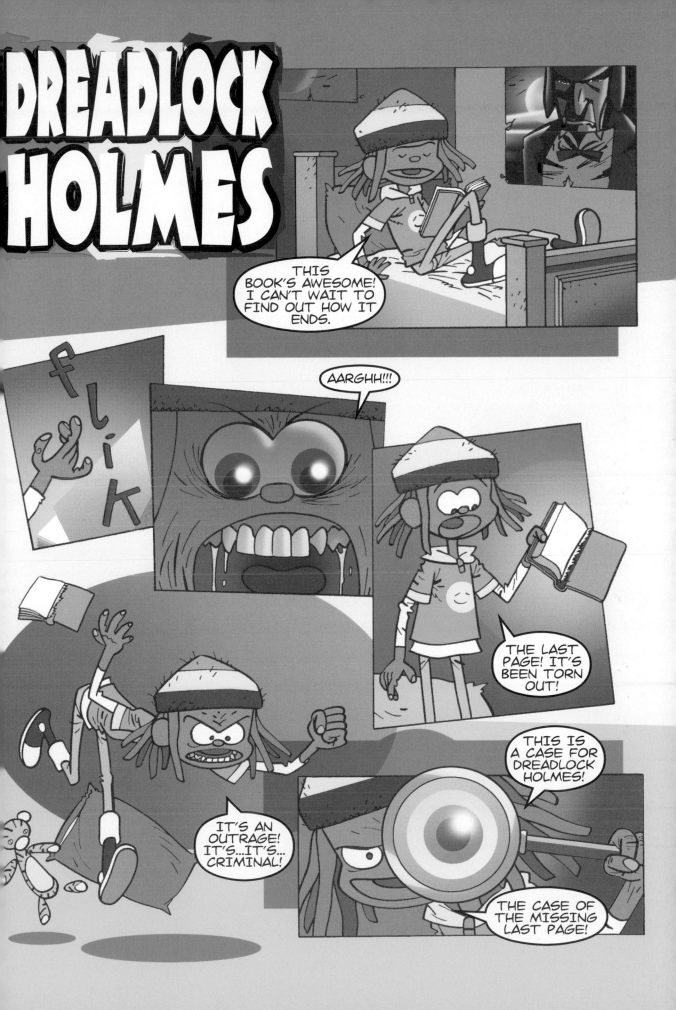

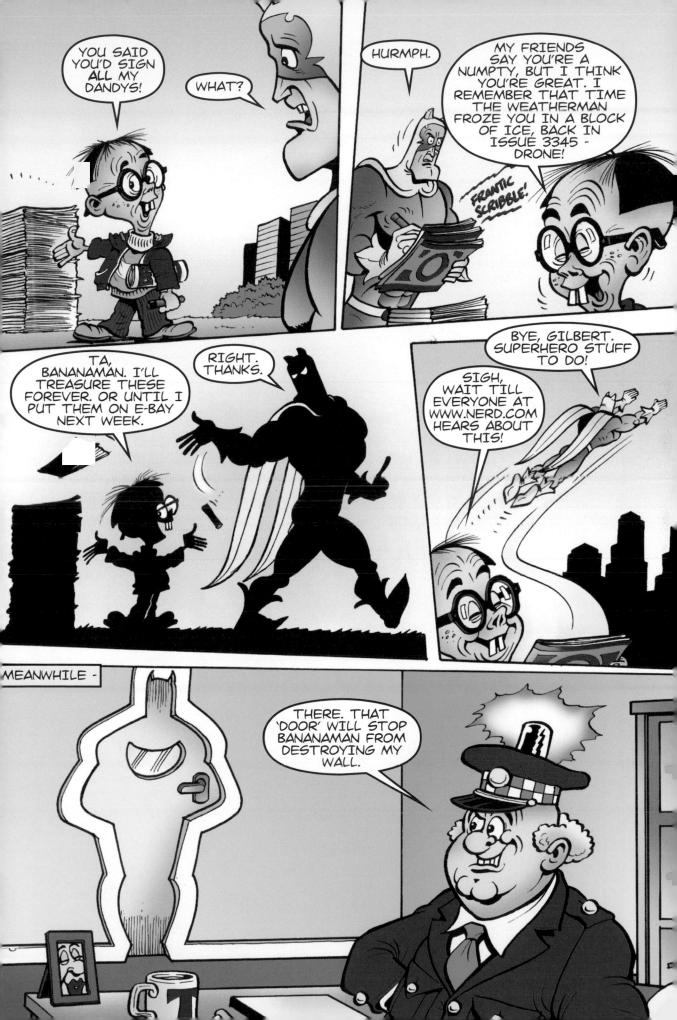

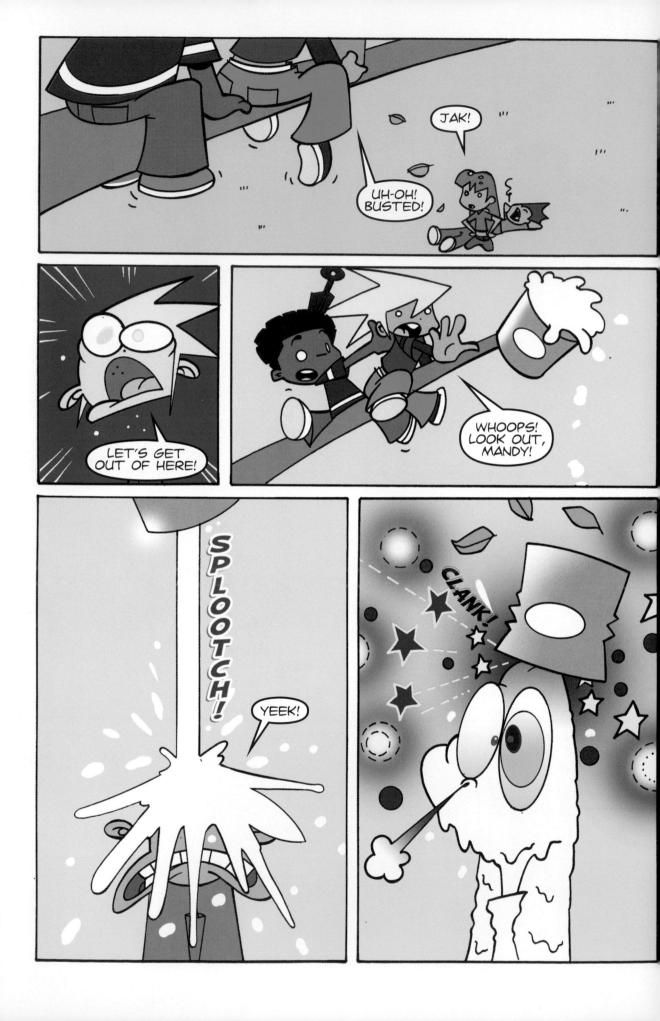

OLLIE FLIPTRIK'S BIG SKATE

The Dandy Skate team have gone to practice... but everyone else has had the same idea. Better try some puzzles while you wait your turn.

WHERE'S OLLIE?
(AND DOUG AND SMUDGER?)
Allow 2 minutes to find them.

Ollie, Doug and Smudger are hidden somewhere in the skatepark.

Take 30 seconds away from your time for every clue you use.

CLUE 1: Ollie is trying to grind a rail (with difficulty).

CLUE 2: It's so busy Doug can't get in!

CLUE 3: Check the half-pipe for Smudger.

MINI-WORDSEARCH
Give yourself 4 minutes to find:
DOUG OLLIE SMUDGER BOARD TRUCK GRIND

Y	G	R	I	N	D	N	I	R	B
P	R	B	T	G	O	L	L	I	E
A	G	E	R	M	U	X	D	B	R
X	S	M	U	D	G	E	R	S	S
G	R	I	C	Z	B	O	A	R	Q
U	R	V	K	M	N	D	O	G	G
O	S	I	J	L	S	D	B	O	A

(TOTALLY) MENTAL MATHS
Allow lots of time for this one.
If you count up the number of skaters,
take away the number of boards and multi-
ply by the number of wheels what do you
get? Don't ask us for the answer, though,
we've lost our calculator!

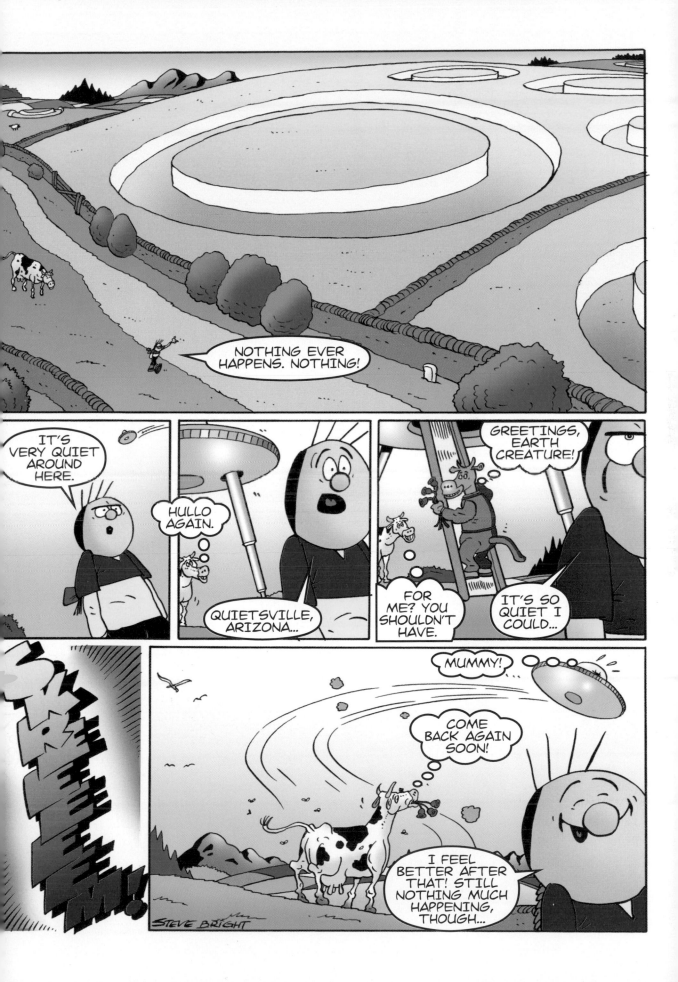

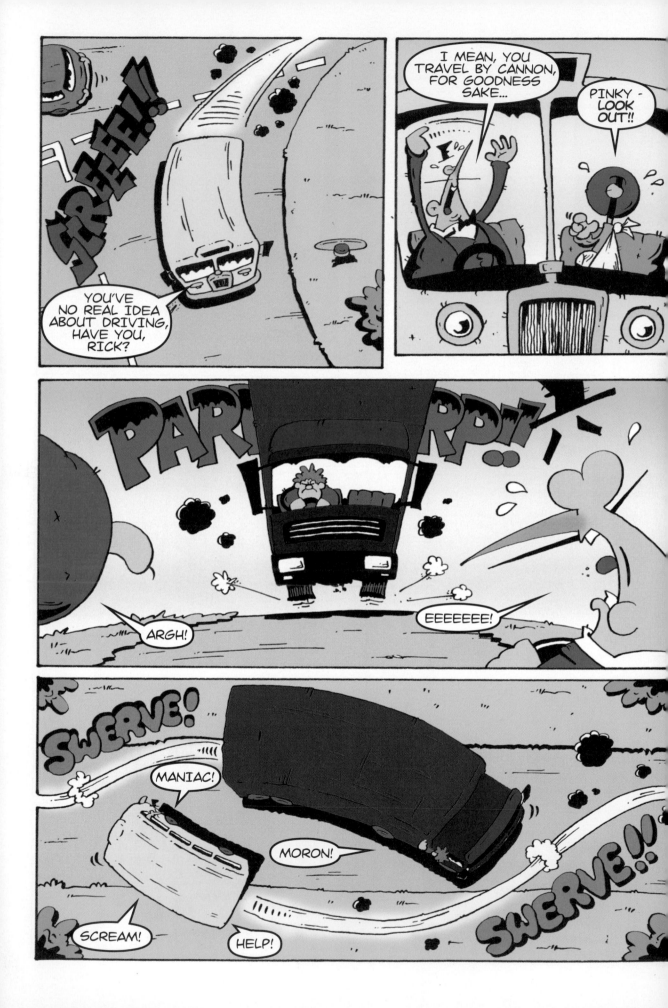

Can ye find these words in amongst the Cap'n's scribblin's?

CANNON
PIRATE
MATE
SCURVY
SPARROW
PLANK
LUBBER
SHIVER
TIMBERS
CAPTAIN

Ye can have five minutes to do this, swab.

AVAST BEHIND!

'Tis piracy on the high seas as Gingerbeard the buccaneer attacks HMS Doolally under the command of Captain Horatio Brennan, RN (he'll be the one with the telescope back to front then...). Now, unless ye want to end up takin' a long walk off a short plank, ye'd better join the pirate crew. Ye'll have to solve these here puzzles to show ye've got pirate blood in yer veins. Oo ar, Jim lad.

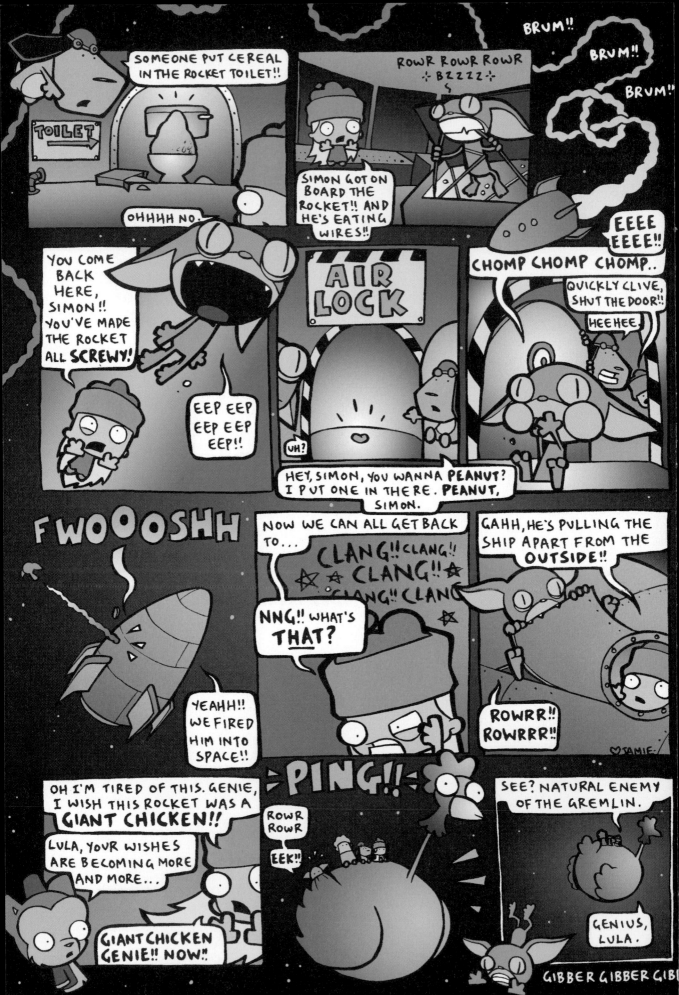

PINKY'S BIG TOP

Welcome to the circus of Pinkerton Gusset the Third. Home of... well, frankly, some of the daftest performers you're ever likely to see. You don't have to be mad to work here, but it does help.

To help you pass the time while you wait for the human cannonball to be rescued from a tree, Pinky has pasted up some puzzles. Ambrose the gorilla did them in 10 minutes. Can you do them faster? (If you can, you might get a job at the circus... but would you want one?!)

TRAVELLING BARBER
PROF: S. TODD

See if you can find these words in the square below (Ambrose said this was tricky because some of the words ran backwards — a bit like Pinky when the lion got out).

CAGE CANNON ELEPHANT WHIP LION
PINKY HORSE BIG TOP RINGMASTER CLOWN

```
O S P A I L A C E Y O N S L N A T P
P A Y Y W T S L N R G H G T I S C R
R E T S A M G N I R N P N I N O E W
A R K O N K I O G E C A O I O C N E
P I A N P I E B H L H L M T N G I P
I S L O L I N I O P K E B T G N O P
N K I A A G I W E N N C A G E I C E
K N W I S N N L S P B O H O N B I N
Y H N R H N E C R I G L O A A I N N
H P M A E G W C O G I H O M I H G N
R C A N N O N H H I L E A S G N A R
W H I P N E T A Y N Y N N W I N C N
```

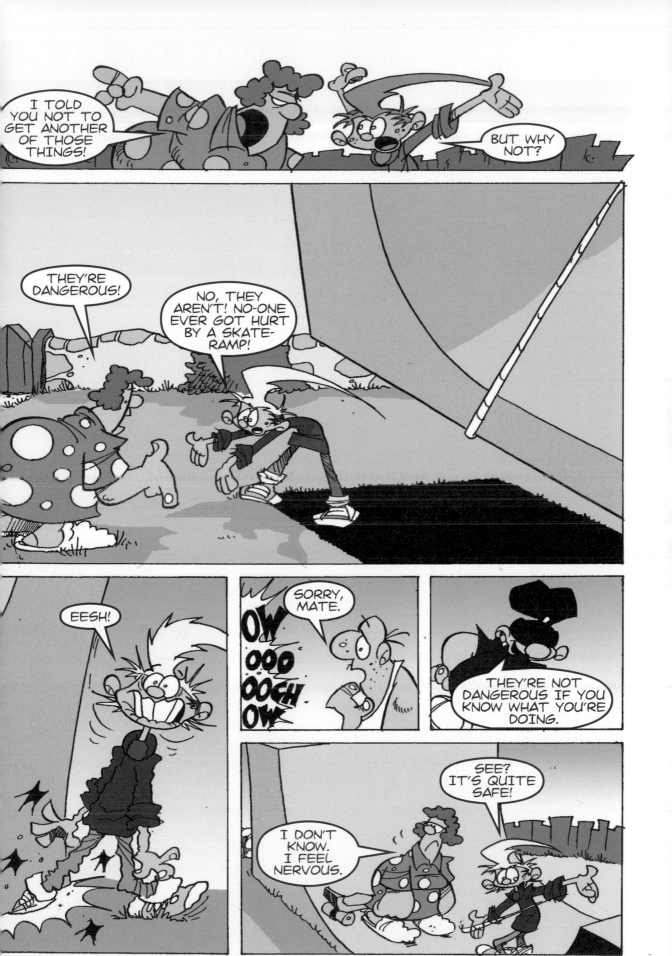

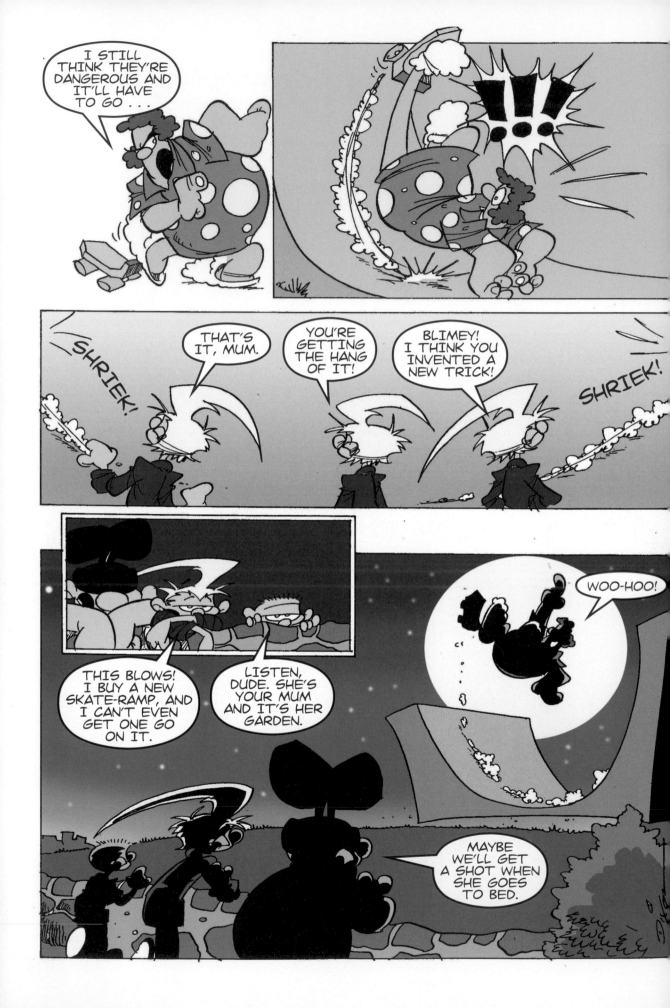

A AERIALS — The name given to any trick where the skateboard and skater leave the ground or a ramp without ollieing.

B BACKSIDE — No, it doesn't mean the thing that you fall on! Oh, all right then, it does.

C CONTUSION — Another word for bruise. If you skate, you're gonna get 'em.

D DECK — The flat bit on the top of a skateboard. Stand here.

e exercise — You get lots of this when skateboarding and it's good for you. So why can't you go skateboarding instead of PE at school?

F FREESTYLE — Skateboarding without ramps or other 'aids' to doing tricks. Also known as flatground skating.

G GRINDS — Tricks where the skateboarder slides on the hangers (the part of the truck that holds the axle which holds the wheels) of the trucks on any object that is smooth enough. Usually performed on handrails or the lips or edges of objects such as benches.

H HELMET — Protective equipment for your head. Nearly always used in vert skateboarding.

i iNDY — The skater reaches his or her back hand down and grabs the toe side of the skateboard between the rider's feet. You can use the same grab in snowboarding but it's a lot colder.

J JAM — Getting a load of skaters together for a skateboard session.

K KICKTUR — Turning a corner c the rear wheels of the board when the front wheels are in the air.

L LEFT — One side of a skateboard, opposite of right.

M MANUAL — Also known as a wheelie. Travelling along on your board on only the two rear wheels.

N NOSE — The part of the deck ahead of the front truck. The opposite e behind the rear truc is called the tail.

O OLLIE — A skateboarding trick where the skateboarder pops the skateboard into the air by kicking the back of the deck. The effect is the skateboarder jumping with the skateboard stuck to his or her feet. Some say Alan "Ollie" Gelfand invented the rolling Ollie in 1977 but our own Mr Fliptrik begs to differ.

P PADS — Protective equipment for the knees and elbows. See contusion for the reason why.

Q QUARTER-PIPE — Basically half a half-pipe. You can use it as a ramp or put two together to make a half-pipe. If the two halfs are put back to back they make a spine ramp.

R REGULAR — Nothing to do with All-Bran! You skate regular if you skate with your left foot forward. You skate goofy if you skate with your right foot forward.

S SKATEBOARD — Come on, pay attention! Do you really need to ask?

T TONY HAWKS — The name on the world's finest skateboard games.

U UPSIDE DOWN — Beginners' boards spend a lot of time like this.

V VERTICAL — Skateboarding using part of an inclined surface that is vertical in gradient. That's straight up and down, so only for experts.

W WHEEL — Your skateboard generally needs four of these things. They come in loads of different shapes, sizes and colours.

X Nothing for X so here's an X-tra W... **Wallie** — Skating onto, up and over a street object. Avoid open-topped bins for this trick.

Y — Yuk! — See above mention of open-topped bins.

Z Zebra — If you see a zebra at the skatepark you've probably fallen on your head once too often. It's time to go home.

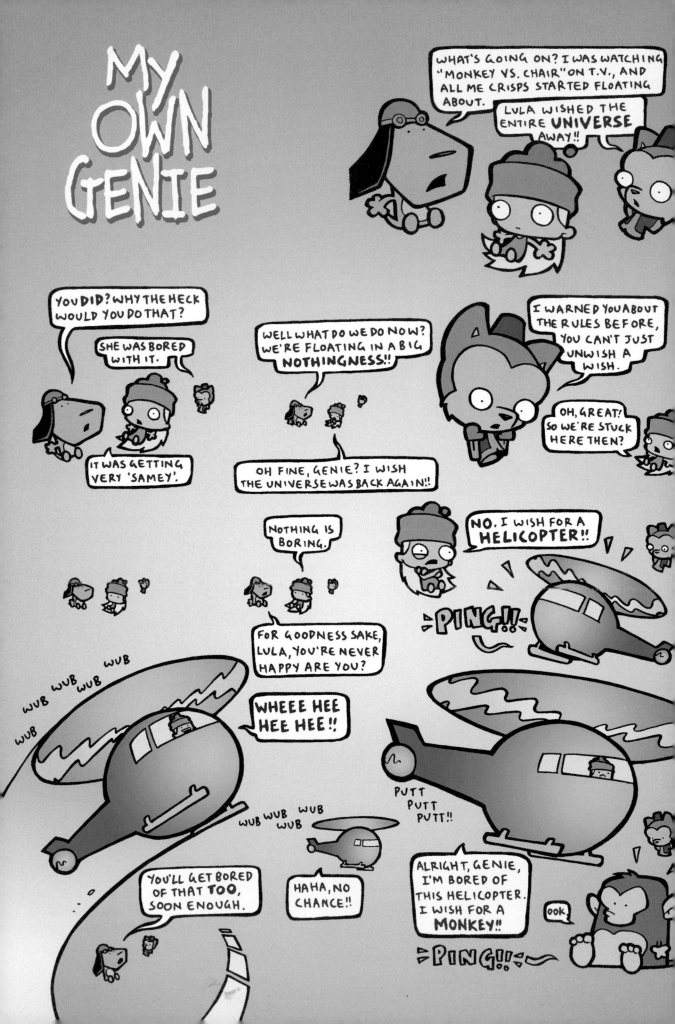

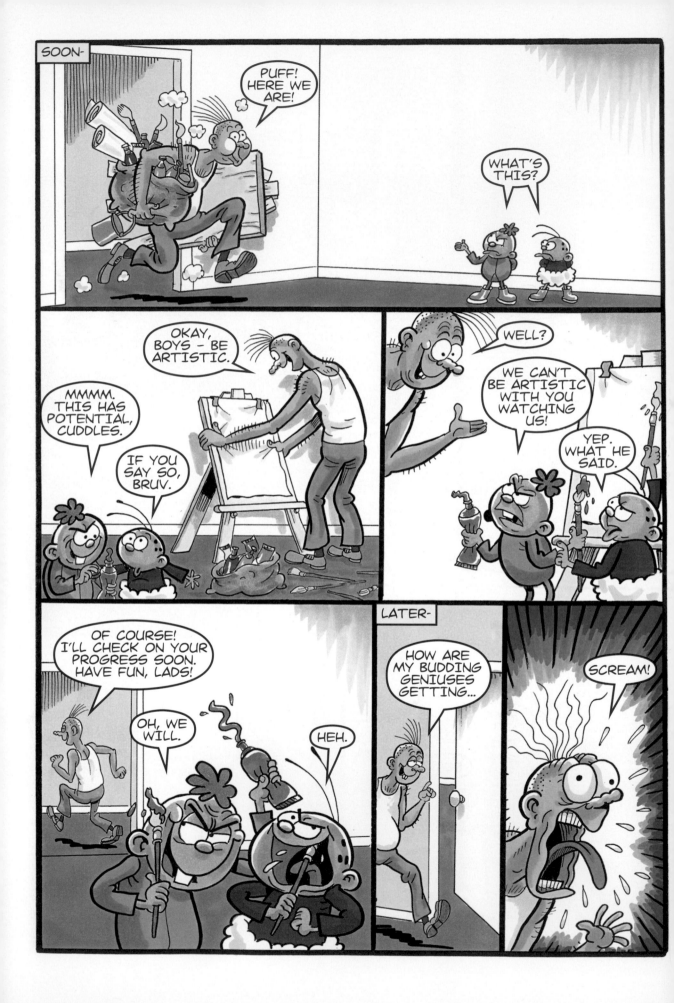